BEYOND THE CLASSROOM

I0793786

# HISTORY IN YOUR LIFE

by Charis Mather

BEARPORT PUBLISHING

Fusion Books, an imprint of Bearport Publishing by FlutterBee

**Credits**

All images are courtesy of Shutterstock.com, unless otherwise specified. With thanks to Getty Images, Thinkstock Photo, and iStockphoto. Cover, © solarus, Line By Line Vectors, Monkey Business Images, Kittyfly, Onica Alexandru Sergiu, Seahorse Vector, NotionPic, Look_Studio, Agus Diantoro, COOL STUFF, Oleksandr Poliashenko, Gorodenkoff. Throughout – Line By Line Vectors, solarus. 4–5, © Elena Vechkanova, imtmphoto; 6–7, © Monkey Business Images, rootstock, frantic00; 8–9, © Halinskyi Max, Reshetnikov_art; 10–11, © LightField Studios, Akarawut, Andrei Porzhezhinskii, Gorodenkoff, SynthEx, indigo_design, the8monkey; 12–13, © Vyaseleva Elena, WESTOCK PRODUCTIONS, Timeless; 14–15, © spass, Thanakorn.P, ClassicVector; 16–17, © antoniodiaz, LightField Studios, BRO.vector; 18–19, © Saad315, SeventyFour; 20–21, © Uncredited DOJ photographer, restored by Adam Cuerden (a relatively minor restoration), Public domain, via Wikimedia Commons, Akkalak Aiempradit/Shutterstock; 22–23, © PeopleImages.com - Yuri A, In Green.

**Bearport Publishing Company Product Development Team**

Kayla Eggert, Theresa Emminizer, Kim Jones, Allison Juda, Cole Nelson, Naomi Reich, Steve Scheluchin, Tiana Tran

Library of Congress Cataloging-in-Publication Data is available at www.loc.gov or upon request from the publisher.

ISBN: 979-8-89577-608-7 (hardcover)
ISBN: 979-8-89577-696-4 (ebook)



For more information, write to Bearport Publishing, 3500 American Blvd W, Suite 150, Bloomington, MN 55431. Printed in the United States of America.

# CONTENTS

# WHAT'S HISTORY GOOD FOR?

Have you ever sat in class and wondered . . .

History is the study of the past. Learning about it helps you understand more about the world and your place in it.

Your life has been shaped by things that happened long before you were born. Let's look at history beyond the classroom!

# HISTORY AROUND US

History is all around you! It's not just in books. History is in pictures, buildings, artwork, and objects that were made long ago.

Look around you. Do you see things from the past?

Sometimes, we can learn about the past in letters or diaries. These are historical **sources**. They show us how people lived and what mattered to them.

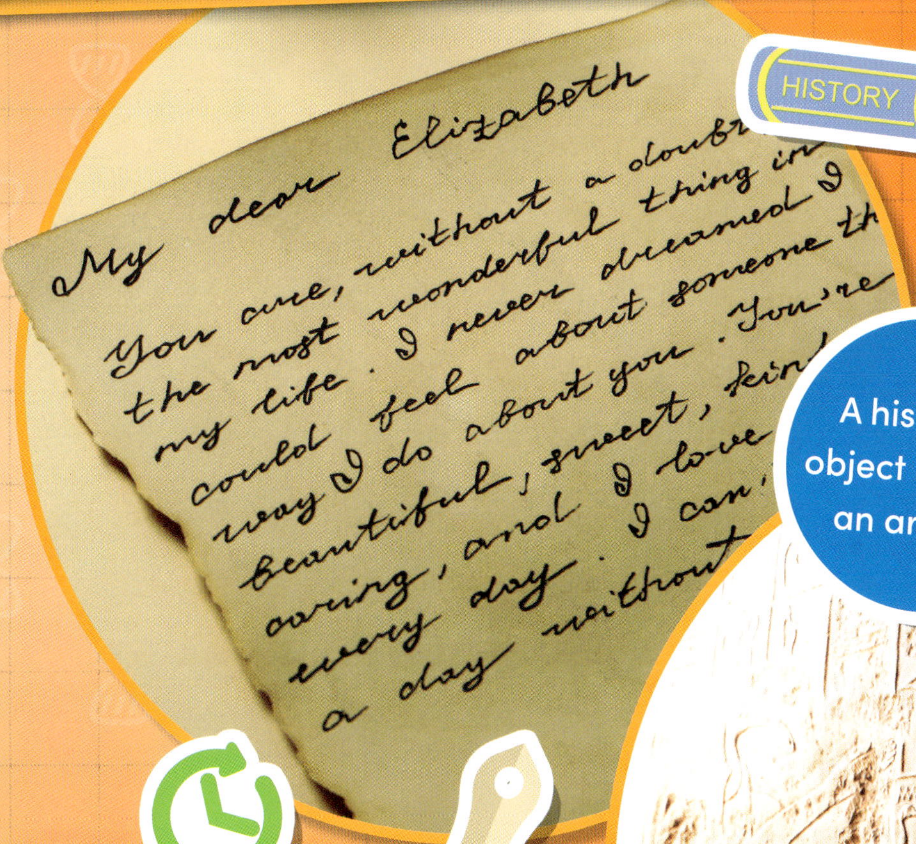


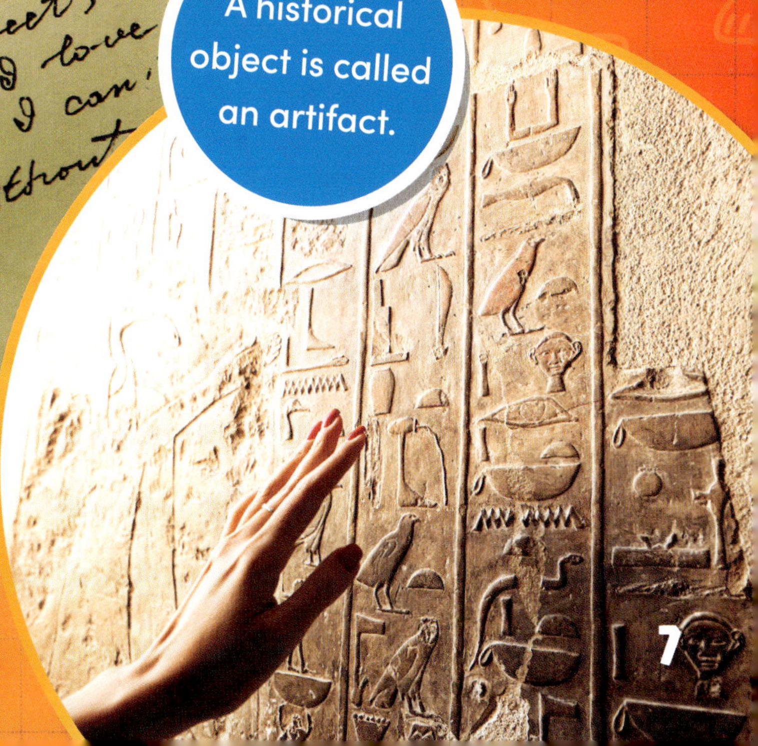

A historical object is called an artifact.

# THINK ABOUT IT!

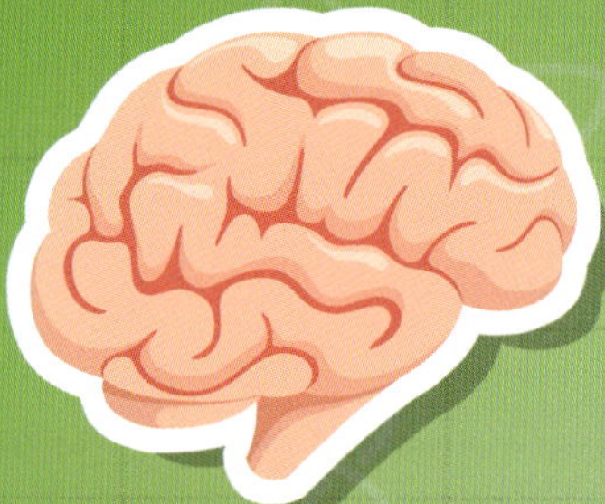

It's important to think carefully about the sources we see. Who made them and why? What were they trying to say or show?

Throughout history, some people's voices have been raised above others. This gives us a limited view of history. We can widen that view by seeking out other **perspectives**.

# HISTORY AT WORK

History is an important part of many jobs.

LIVE

Journalists record history in real time!

Tour guides bring history to life by showing people important places from the past.

Researchers dig deep into the past to understand how people used to live.

**Archaeologists** study historical **sites** and objects.

Museum workers take care of historical artifacts.

Lawyers, writers, teachers, and filmmakers use history, too!

# FAMILY HISTORY

Without historical records, it would be much harder to keep track of people's families. By collecting and studying historical records, we can find out a lot about the people who lived before us.

The study of family history is called genealogy (*jee-nee-AL-uh-jee*).

Learning about your family history can help you get to know yourself better. It may explain why your family lives in a certain place or has certain **traditions**.

Family trees show how family members are connected.

# IDENTITY AND CULTURE

History can also help us understand culture. Culture is the shared traditions, beliefs, and ways of life of a group of people. This can be an important part of someone's **identity**.

People celebrate culture in lots of fun ways. We might wear special clothing, make music, dance, or eat food. This helps us connect to our culture and one another.

How do you celebrate your culture?

# PERSPECTIVE

Have you ever been in a disagreement with someone about how something happened? You might have wished that the other person could see your side of the story.

**Bias** is a personal view of something. It is not based on facts.

Studying history teaches you how to look at events from different perspectives. Thinking about how different people may have experienced the same event can help you understand what happened better.

# RECORDING KNOWLEDGE

Written records help us keep track of information. Without records, people would have to keep figuring out the same things over and over again!

Lots of what we know about science, math, and languages comes from historical records.

As with other kinds of sources, it's important to think about who wrote historical records. Are the facts presented clearly and without bias?

# LOOKING FORWARD

Learning about history can help us learn from mistakes others made. This can help us make different choices in the future.

Ruby Bridges was part of a historic change to make schools more fair. We learn her story so we can do better now.

Knowing more about the past helps us understand why the world is different today. History can help us build a better future.

# PRACTICING HISTORY

We can learn a lot from the past. It can help us find out more about who we are and who we want to be!

How was life in the past different from your life today?

Why not try asking people in your life about their pasts? They might have some interesting or important stories to tell you. Or you could write about or look at pictures from your own past! History goes way beyond the classroom!

# GLOSSARY

**archaeologists** scientists who dig up and study old objects to learn about people from the past

**bias** support for only one side of a situation

**identity** a person's view of who they are

**perspectives** points of view

**sites** places where things are

**sources** where things come from or information is found

**traditions** the beliefs, customs, or ways of behaving that have been around for a long time

# INDEX